COMMISERATIONS

Written and
Illustrated by
Cathy Guisewite

Andrews and McMeel
A Universal Press Syndicate Company
Kansas City

ISBN: 0-8362-3048-5

COMMISERATIONS

Don't judge a woman
until you've walked a
mile in her open-toed,
sling-back, spike-heeled
platform pumps.

Which is worse,
that I hear the
refrigerator ringing
or that it has
Call Waiting?

Why do the right words
always come out of the
wrong mouth?

I want a man who
does to my heart what
chocolate does to
my brain.

I won't be in today.
My hair won't start.

The only men I really
communicate with are
the ones I'll never
speak to again.

Only love can
break a heart,
but a shoe sale
can come close.

SALE

SIZE 5

SIZE 6½

SIZE 7

SIZE 13

How much more lingerie must I buy before I own my womanhood?

We are never so sure
of ourselves as when
we're rejecting
everything we own.

I have met his mistress,
and she wears a little
sock on her head.

I haven't learned
to let go, but I'm
getting better at
losing my grip.

For some, life is a
journey. For me, it's
72,000 individual trips.

The only time I ever
listen to my body is
when it tells me to do
something I'll regret.

When a man transforms
his life it always involves
a beautiful woman.

When I do it, it involves
little cartons of crunchy
vegetables.

It isn't smog.
It's eyeshadow.

The problem with
microwave dinners
is that while the stomach
has had a nice, full meal,
the brain is only 7.2
minutes into dinner
hour.

Seventy-five
relationship books,
200 magazine articles,
and 1,000 sultry outfits
later, and the only truly
alluring thing I've ever
done was to leave.

Make the world
a better place to live.
Stay in bed.

Never underestimate
the power of going for a
day without makeup.

Life is passing me by,
and it has such
little feet.

I'm surrounded by
idiots and I'm the only
one in the office.

Beauty is always
the first to go, but vanity
is always the last
to leave.

If the emotional
baggage doesn't trash
the relationship, the
carry-on luggage will.

If men's hair falls out
it's because there's
nothing in there for it
to hang onto.

I have it all,
and I carry it all
with me.

There's one special
man for all of us.
<u>One</u> man for <u>all</u> of us.

We always find the
strength to do the one
thing that will make
us feel worse.

Sometimes I
think they call it a
relationship because we
have to keep redoing it
so many times.

All men are created equal. All women are created superior.

a garden, as near as possible to the sky, was the way of the Cherkess. Undoubtedly we were the healthier for it. One of my most vivid childhood memories is the icy thrill of cold sheets on foggy nights, followed by the blissful sensation of drifting into sleep as the bed warmed up. We rose and retired with the sun.

Early among educators, the Jesuits were charged with believing that a child was formed or deformed by the age of eight. In my life certainly those years determined what was to follow, though I might argue that the Jesuits' allowance of time was too handsome by half. Adventuring from the cozy cocoon of infancy in a loving family, I quickly discovered the enchantment of natural sounds. I can have been no older than two or three when a first awareness of nature was given me by the crowing of a rooster. A homely bird enough, to bear the weight of interest in nonhuman creation, farming, conservation and ecology that my life has since laid upon him; but his voice sounds yet with the exuberance in being alive that I first responded to all those years ago. Although I must in fact have heard roosters in the short time we spent with my uncle, my memory fixes them not there, but on another farm, at Walnut Creek, owned by another Russian-Jewish family, called Kavin. Mr. Kavin, a tall man with red hair and beard, had a docile little wife and two daughters, particular friends of mine named Ida and Zena, with whom I built houses of wooden crates to hide in.

Another early memory is falling in love. From the earliest age I was always fond of girls, always in love with someone about whom I wove romances, up to whose image I lived, without saying anything about it. The first of this procession of girls was a toddler called Lili, met when we lived in Berkeley. Perhaps I was too young to conceal my passion, but however that may be, my parents cynically exploited it to ensure my good behavior. "Lili's asleep," they would reproach me, in the hope that I would be chastened into following suit, and thoroughly taken in, I would resign myself to the day's ending with lullabies about my love: *"Lili alcha lichon"*—"Lili's gone to sleep." For in those days Hebrew was still the language of the house. Overhearing one such cradle chant, a visiting friend from San Francisco, Reuben Rinder, himself a cantor in the temple, thought it evidence of musical talent and a couple of years later encouraged Aba and Imma to take my ambitions seriously. I am sure the word of a professional singer carried weight.

Both my parents were linguists, Imma notably so, and both spoke English before coming to the United States. Until I was three, how-

the temple, and, indeed, represented as incendiary rather than sacerdotal, as a force of destruction or creation rather than a light from beyond the grave. If Sammy Marantz, fifty years later, still recalls Bialik's poem about the pogrom of Kichinev, "The City of Slaughter," in which he reproaches Jews for their meekness, such history as my father taught must have been martial and apocalyptic, calculated to recruit pioneers rather than parishioners. Like Nicholas of Cologne marshaling children for the Children's Crusade, he held forth an image of Jerusalem waiting to be captured by the young. That Nicholas was to become the legendary Pied Piper of Hamelin and Jerusalem Venusberg only underlines my parallel: my father prepared his pupils for a rite of passage very different in spirit from the official confirmation. Where the latter celebrates puberty and inducts a young man into the adult tribe, he urged them to join a tribe without elders, implying that on the far side of Bar Mitzvah lay not adjustment, but ecstatic renovation, not the humdrum world round about them, but a land of exquisite sentiments and valorous feats. When the text of the Balfour Declaration reached Elizabeth soon after our arrival, it made my father appear, in his pupils' eyes, its prophetic emissary. Sammy Marantz wrote a poem whose title, "At Last! At Last!", suggests that two months of Menuhin tutelage could generate as many millennia of longing in a twelve-year-old.

Never did my parents doubt that where they stood was anything other than a secure place to stand. Such assurance has immense power of attraction, but I doubt that it was only this which made them alluring to children. My mother in particular could not see a young person without wanting to weld him or her into the family, an urge she has never lost and which she has handed down to my sister Hephzibah. Sammy Marantz was, to my knowledge, the first to prompt it, and to such effect that he has remained an adopted member of the family ever since. On snowy winter evenings he would load a sled with firewood and pickled green tomatoes fished from his family's barrels like Jewish valentines, and haul it to our house on Julia Street. It was a symbolic exchange: he brought wood and sweetmeats; he sought warmth and the spiritual provender my parents alone were capable of feeding him. Some six years later Sammy was suddenly to appear at our door in San Francisco, having enrolled at Berkeley; hardly was he in the house before he sat down to read *Ivanhoe* with me. A couple of years later still, when he was back at home and we were marooned, temporarily fatherless, in New York, he would often come to lighten the gloom of banishment. By his youthful devotion I can estimate my parents' impact on the children of Elizabeth—by that, and by what happened when my parents suddenly left town.

The children's excitement had not escaped the rabbi's notice, nor his disapproval. Not that he was a cruel man, it's safe to guess, but guilt, exile and lamentation being his stock in trade, he could not stand by and see an enterprise so richly dour cheered into bankruptcy. He defended his closed universe against my parents' attempts to let in light and air. Their weapon was ardor, his red tape, but before battle could be truly joined, a newspaper item about California caught my father's eye and in the space of a morning grew to a vision and decided our future. The arrangements for leaving took scarcely longer.

Directly our flight became known, the *Talmud Torah* class staged a revolt and, with the same instinct that tells grown-up insurgents to occupy the National Archives and the Civil Registry, confiscated the school records. Naïvely the rabbi offered them bags of candy, then, as they were not to be bribed into submission, dismissed them from the school. My parents had bequeathed a sense of the messianic, but left no doctrine and arranged no apostolic succession among their twelve-year-old followers. Believers without tangible support for their faith, they drifted home and in time, one supposes, fell disconsolately into line.

We meanwhile had got as far as Grand Central Station and discovered that the cheapest journey, a patchwork of stops and starts on local trains, cost fifteen dollars more than we could muster. "Don't you worry," said a generous ticket clerk, taking pity on our dashed hopes. "I'll make the money up." Thus my first benefactor, whose memory and whose good American heart I salute: where would one find his like today? A week later we arrived in California.

I was four years old before Hephzibah was born and five and a half before Yaltah's birth completed the family. To have sisters, especially loving and admiring ones, is an experience I unreservedly recommend (a brother would perhaps have challenged my position). I believe, however, that just as I was eventually enriched by sisters, I was earlier enriched by four years of my parents' undivided love. It seems, looking back, that we were never separated, Aba ("father" in Hebrew), Imma ("mother") and myself. There is some truth in the recollection, for during the Elizabethan interlude my parents apparently carried me in a big basket-cot to the *Talmud Torah* to have

me under their eye while they taught, but clearly there must [been many times when work took Aba away. So strong is my im]sion of security and happiness, however, it has submerged h[sences entirely. One of several images sums up the early days i]fornia: I am being toted on Aba's shoulders, Imma is walking us, we are all three together and have nothing left to wish f above all nothing to fear.

A telegram to Aba's brother who owned a chicken farm n[Francisco had preceded us to California, bringing my uncle us at Oakland Pier, where the trains stopped. A few days or w the chicken farm followed, but Imma's character not being for dependence, we soon moved to Berkeley. After some weeks or months there, Aba was appointed a teacher of He the San Francisco Jewish community at a salary of $150 a and we moved across the bay to an apartment at 732 Hay[Here we were to remain until I was six, when with two litt added to our number, one just walking, the other in her cr modest apartment was coming undone at the seams and we house of our own.

If my sensibility finds itself nowhere more at home than nant wooden chamber whose walls curve round a sound p organized to begin with in a tent. Imma's fancy ran t coasts, unpeopled views. Halfway around the globe from Sea to the shores of the Pacific she followed an itinerary until she found in vertiginous, sea-surrounded San sufficient reason to make a pause. But her longing for ai dom could not be satisfied with mere views through wind ever noble, or mere excursions, however taxing, and so it that no sooner had we moved into Hayes Street than we again, in a manner of speaking. Abutting the windows wa upon which an awning was pitched and there, if the weat way suitable, we slept. Four years later, when the house Street was bought, the arrangements for escaping confin less provisional. A porch or small bungalow, separate fro was built in the garden, consisting of a wooden frame roof and walls to waist height, above which were nettin side, the structure was divided into two halves, one for the other further divided into a larger room for Hephzi tah and a smaller one for me. There was common sens Extra rooms were gained and a floor liberated for lodg omy was not the prime impetus behind it. To bivouac o

ever, they did not speak English to me; our family unity was expressed in a family language. I am only sorry that English was introduced before I had a chance to master reading and writing in Hebrew. Its sound is still in my ears and I have, for instance, broadcast in Hebrew, but only with a script written in phonetic letters and the proper emphases indicated. The early fluency is lost, and the words I recall tend to cluster round the physiological interests of a three-year-old, such words as *regel,* "leg," or *beten,* "stomach," probably much used in connection with aches and bruises as excuses for getting attention. After the transfer to English, Hebrew remained a household code for instructions to do this or that or be quiet and mind one's manners which outsiders were not meant to understand. Neither of my sisters had my Hebrew opportunities, but thereafter in our pursuit of languages—of which there were to be several—we all three hunted together. Indeed, they went further than I.

Although neither of my parents spoke Yiddish to us children, both understood it and Aba spoke it fluently. Somewhat later in my boyhood, lying in bed on my side of the partition in the Steiner Street garden house, I would hear him read the works of Sholom Aleichem to my mother, and every so often a burst of laughter would reach me. Those were moments of happiness for all of us. To me, awake in the dark, they meant there was complete harmony in the household. Not that disharmony was otherwise the rule: on the contrary, so dependent were my parents on each other and so well-established their different functions—my father responsible for anything of a breadwinning or practical nature, my mother for keeping house and for the children's morals and education—there was no opportunity for dissension. But Sholom Aleichem provided occasion for a drop from high purpose into light-heartedness. So elevated was Imma's conception of existence, it was as if she were living an ideal script, handed down by her ancestors and pinned to some lofty level by her own self-discipline. I use an image from the stage deliberately, for someone who never capitulates to pain or sloth impresses us as heeding a greater power than his own, as the actor does; in the wings, however, the actor lets the illusion go, but Imma never did, for so far from illusion were her convictions, they penetrated every depth of her character.

She liked things to be seen in their global unity. An outing was not simply an outing, but had its moral and spiritual as well as its physical aspects; a holiday had its quota of related study; enjoyment was taken in awareness of other people who were not so privileged. She would relate with approval a little drama from her own childhood:

given a new dress for a party, she was in a state of high excitement when her mother said, "Look, I know you love your new dress, but there are many children who don't have pretty clothes. Wouldn't you feel much better if you went to the party in your old dress and gave this one away?" From my own early years I recall an event less stern in its demands but equally rounded in its implications. This was my first excursion alone with her—memorable on that account, if for no other reason, for, three-year-old child though I was, she filled me with chivalrous self-importance by entrusting me with the responsibility of escorting her. Secondly, we went to Napa County, a beautiful agricultural part of California. Last but not least, our journey had moral justification because our purpose was to visit a patient in a mental hospital. I remember scarcely anything of the outing except an institution with great gates and a general notion of this poor man's pitiful case, but the lesson was implanted that pleasure had its debt to pay. As I have said, she identified with prisoners of every sort, but especially the "visionary" for whom the real world lay elsewhere. In Jaffa she had gone for a time to a school run by nuns, and retained a respect for those who renounce everything to serve others (in contrast, she was dubious about priests, rabbis, or anyone who made a profession of being godly). Her own life was one of renunciation, of course, requiring the sacrifice of assets more considerable than party dresses, such as freedom and fulfillment.

We were still at Hayes Street and I by now old enough to notice that my father went to work each day, when a Dutch windmill in a toyshop window caught my fancy. Our regular morning walk took us past the toyshop to a neighborhood park, but custom did not stale, but rather reinforced, the windmill's appeal. Here again Imma found occasion to link reward with purpose: when I could pronounce an *r* without lisping evasion of its difficulty, the toy would be mine. I knew exactly how an *r* should sound, but my wretched tongue was not nimble enough to deliver itself of this impossible consonant, clearly invented for another anatomy than mine. Valiantly, day and night, in corners, I practiced, and now became clear the usefulness of sleeping in a tent apart from the house. With my infant sisters abed and asleep before me, and my parents still up and about for a few hours yet, I was left at liberty to concentrate on rolling at my target. Then, one evening when Aba and Imma had just gone to bed, I knew I had it. What to do? If I wakened them in the middle of the night, they would hardly be pleased; if I waited until morning, my tongue might have forgotten its skill. With my head under the bedclothes, I tested myself surreptitiously at intervals through the night and when dawn was breaking, raised the household with a superb "rrrrr!" And got my windmill. (I hesitate to find any deep significance in the episode, but it is nonetheless true that over half a century later, I have renewed my interest in windmills, and will preach them at anyone who cares to listen as the conservationist's electric generator.)

But I have still not done my mother justice. If, on the one hand, she gave shape to existence by her exalted idea of it, on the other she had the knack of the delightful surprise. She used the bonds of duty as much to fasten down her own temperament as to provide guidelines for her children's growing up, I am sure. That she had a wild spirit capable of devastating eruption was not in doubt, but so perfect was her control that one only ever glimpsed its reflection or caught its echo. Solely in the matter of pleasure, of picnics, holidays, interruptions of the agenda, would she unleash the unpredictable, spontaneous side of her nature; but then totally. She could not—still cannot —endure to have the savoring of existence blighted by prudence. It was Aba's inclination to foresee eventualities and prepare to meet them. In the ordinary course of events, this was accepted and acted upon, but if Aba's forethought trespassed on leisure, Imma would say, half warning, half ironical, "Moshe! P-p-p-plans!" and timetables would be cast to the winds in the cause of adventure.

Such holidays, overturning routine with delightful unexpectedness, were to be a feature of my childhood and youth. Naturally, when my sisters were still infants and the family still confined to public transport, enterprises of this daring character were beyond our scope, but I can't remember a time when pleasure outings didn't enliven our weeks like so many bursts of sunshine. There were Sunday picnics—a very San Franciscan diversion in those days. There were visits to the rural Kavins and to the Kayes, a prosperous tradesman's family in Berkeley. In return, my parents entertained at home. And from before my conscious memory records the fact, there was music.

In 1918, when I was two, my parents smuggled me into a matinee concert of the San Francisco Symphony Orchestra, and no misadventure occurring to dissuade them, regularly continued the contraband operation until I was old enough to have a ticket on my own account. In after years Imma let it be known that Aba and she had taken me with them because they couldn't afford a baby-sitter. No doubt baby-sitters were a luxury in their struggling young lives, but this granted, I have my reservations about the story. It was characteristic of her to puncture myth with a deft injection of matter of fact.

It was no less characteristic to hold that the earlier an experience, the more valuable. When my sisters were expected, I remember her conviction that the life she led, the music she heard, the thoughts she had, were part and parcel of the environment of the coming baby, a subject now for theses by learned doctors, but to her simply a truth. So much the more forcibly must she have believed that as soon as I could be trusted not to disgrace myself, I should be allowed to share what she and Aba delighted in. In view of my future connection with concerts, it might justly be argued that it was rather I who took them; but my own interpretation of the facts concealed by the high cost of baby-sitters is based on the happiness of my early years. So sure is the memory of my being the apple of my parents' eyes, I can't believe they ever entertained the idea of going to a concert and leaving me behind. We went to concerts, as we did most things, together.

While I don't claim to remember the very first concert, a powerful recollection of the repeated experience remains with me. Seated on Imma's knee in the gallery, I am looking over a shadowy cliff, as through a telescope the wrong way round, at the bottom of which the musicians in a pool of light are miniature but distinct, their busy concentration down there producing sounds to ravish soul and sense.

This ravishment I owe to a ponderous edifice called the Curran Theatre, where the orchestra then played. As if that were not debt enough, the Curran put me under further obligation, providing additional sustenance for an imagination stimulated by music. Every year the Pantages Vaudeville Company would come to San Francisco, and every time it came, I was taken to marvel at the acrobats, clowns, conjurers and dancers, and to be enchanted anew by the first solo violinist ever to impress me, a swarthy fellow called Carichiarto, who had a regular slot in the program and played quite beautifully. Knowing somehow that my world did not begin and end in San Francisco, sensing in my mother the exotic East, feeling drawn to great distances myself, I was bound to confer reality on this magical world, and in time and in turn, to find my violin a theatre; for this box would prove spacious enough to hold jugglers, dancers, a Tartar horde, gypsies, souks, caravanseries, houris, in fact all of paradise. But no single experience of the theatre more lastingly marked me than a performance by Anna Pavlova. Twice, in fact, I saw her dance, the earliest occasions I remember of being absolutely carried away; hardly less transporting was the mere sight of her luggage. One morning in Geary Street, at the stage entrance to the Curran Theatre, we came across six or seven great wardrobe trunks, packed no doubt with her costumes and those of the *corps de ballet* and awaiting collection at the conclusion of her one-night stand. This image of the traveling artist affected me so deeply that I remember it yet with some flicker of my youthful excitement. On stage she would include in her program "The California Poppy," a dance which celebrated a favorite flower of mine, one I would long for in the years away from California, but vainly, for it flourished wild only in my home state, and there it grew everywhere in spring. Delicate, orange, sweet-smelling, the California poppy has a peculiarly touching manner of closing in upon itself as it droops; thus ended Pavlova's dance.

I lost my heart to her. Forsaking Lili and Lili's successors, I dreamed only of Pavlova for many many months, and though I did not see her dance a third time, nor ever meet her, the dream endured. Sown in a sensibility fashioned by my mother, the seed Pavlova planted, a conception of beauty and grace perfected by the discipline of the dance, was to come to flower in adult life in my wife, Diana.

2

A Chevrolet and
a Half-Size Violin

Perched high on the Curran Theatre cliff on concert afternoons, I let my gaze slide past the conductor, whose part in the delightful goings-on below rather defeated my comprehension, to focus on the concert-master, Louis Persinger. Once in a while he would have a solo passage. I learned to wait for those moments when the sweet, lovely sound of the violin floated up to the gallery, thrilling, caressing, and more entrancing than any other. During one such performance I asked my parents if I might have a violin for my fourth birthday and Louis Persinger to teach me to play it.

If this narrative has taken its time to relate a detail which earlier accounts have furnished straightaway, it is to undo the impression that I was shapeless protoplasm one day and myself the next, that musical gift comes to light with the *éclat* of the transformation scene in a pantomime. The finger I pointed at Louis Persinger could base its choice on four years that had given me what as many years of college rarely give the graduate: a sense of vocation. Is this particular sense native to childhood itself? I wonder. Have the fortunate simply rescued from an otherwise lost age of innocence the conviction of un-limited possibility, the instinct for real worth, which make it easier for children to identify with great soloists or simple souls than with able middlemen? Certainly, looking at children from an adult perspective, I have long believed that the grown-up world consistently underrates the young, finding marvels in ambition and achievement where none exists. At the age of four I was too young to know that the violin would exact a price commensurate with the grace it conferred—the grace of flying, of occupying an absolute vantage point, of enjoying such dominion over nerve, bone and muscle as could render the body an ecstatic absentee. But I did know, instinctively, that to play was to be.

Quite simply I wanted to be Persinger, and with equal straightforwardness proposed the means of bringing this enviable situation about. I don't think my parents found my request far-fetched—Aba's childhood had set a precedent, after all—but they may have found it more whimsical than urgent, and hesitated to invest any of their small resources in what might prove to be a child's caprice. As events were to show, they retailed my plea to friends and relations, in the manner of fond parents everywhere, and as a consequence I acquired in turn a toy fiddle and a real one.

I shall never forget the disappointment of that imitation violin. Made of metal, with metal strings, cold to the touch, with a sound as horribly tinny as its construction, this travesty of my longings enraged me for, as far as I recall, the first time in my life. The setting of its presentation and my ungracious reception of it was a large, beautiful park on a hill at the top of Steiner Street, a park whose lawns and thickets were to become very familiar to my sisters and myself a couple of years later. Seated with Aba and Imma on a bench was a fellow teacher from Aba's school who there and then gave me his present. The poor man must have been taken aback when, getting no response from the toy, I burst into sobs, threw it on the ground and would have nothing more to do with it. I am sorry that my first patron in the matter of violins should have been so dustily rewarded for his kindness. I could not know that for myself gratification was only postponed.

Gratification was assured shortly thereafter by a check for eight hundred dollars sent by my Grandmother Sher in Palestine, who had been told of my musical inclinations and had sufficient vision, or generosity, or recklessness, to take them seriously. Wisely my parents decided that half of this very considerable sum was enough to spend on a beginner's violin, and diverted the rest toward the cost of our first car. I can't now determine which purchase added more to my happiness.

I might have met my grandmother but for Aba's anguish at the thought of being separated, however provisionally, from his wife. About the time of my grandmother's gift to us there was a plan that she should travel from Jaffa and Imma should travel from America, with the newly born Hephzibah and me in tow, to a reunion in Italy. It collapsed under the weight of Aba's distress, to remain ever after a sorrowful reminder to him of the sacrifice he had demanded of Imma rather than make himself. For Imma never saw her mother again. One morning, when I was six or seven and we were already living in Steiner Street, she woke up with a dreadful certainty that her mother had died. So heavy was her premonition that Aba sent a telegram to Jaffa, and when no answer, either good or bad, had come by the next day, rang the telegraph office. The dread news had in fact arrived, but the clerks couldn't bring themselves to pass it on. Thus solemnly and eerily was I made aware of the first irreversible event of my life.

With Grandmother Sher's death, our closest bond with Palestine had gone. Dutifully Aba still wrote to an older sister there, but as he was not fond of this particular sister, and indeed blamed her for his younger sister's unhappy love affair ending in suicide, Imma persuaded him, rather determinedly, that his dutifulness was mere hypocrisy, and the correspondence ceased. He was probably the easier to persuade in that Imma's arguments coincided with his own repudiation of his last Zionist loyalties, a decision which left him a confirmed anti-Zionist thereafter. But it was neither the one allegiance nor the other that motivated my mother. In her vision, her best gift to her children was a life emancipated from all restrictions, claims and inhibitions of the past, a world in which they belonged.

Our new car, a little open four-door Chevrolet, might have stood symbol for the freedom my mother desired for us. It had a personality and a name to go with it, which to my shame I no longer remember, and we all loved it extravagantly. Without roof or windows, it offered an airy journey unblemished by fumes. I actually liked the smell of gasoline in those days, before lead was put into it. In the morning, with the just risen sun warming the gas, the faint odor intoxicatingly conjured up the landscapes we would shortly be exploring, and affected Aba no less powerfully than myself. Our journeys always spurred him into song, the refuge for the emotional abandon he too often denied himself. He was a careful driver, never exceeding fifteen miles an hour in our first year of car ownership, then venturing as far as eighteen while holding those who overtook us at twenty to be reckless adventurers without thought for the lives of their families or of anyone else on the road. It took us four hours to